STARTERS

Teeth

Saviour Pirotta

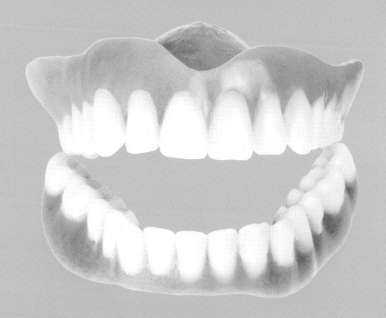

an imprint of Hodder Children's Books

Text copyright © Saviour Pirotta 2003

Language consultant: Andrew Burrell
Design: Perry Tate Design

Published in Great Britain in 2003
by Hodder Wayland, an imprint of
Hodder Children's Books

The publishers would like to thank the following for allowing us to reproduce their
pictures in this book: Science Photo Library; cover, 4 (top), 5 (bottom), 6-7, 9 (top),
11 (top), 15, 17, 19 (bottom), 21, 23 (top), 24 (top 3 pictures) / Bruce Coleman; 4
(bottom), 5 (top), 7 (left), 10, 11 (bottom), 12, 24 (bottom) / Hodder Wayland picture
library; 8, 13 (top), 18, 22 / Oxford Scientific Films; 13 (bottom), 16 (bottom) /
Heather Angel; 16 (top) / Family Life Picture Library; 19 (top), 23 (bottom) / James
Davis Travel Photography; 9 (bottom) / Martyn Chillmaid; title page, contents page,
14, 20

A Catalogue record for this book is available from the British Library.

ISBN: 0750243600

Printed and bound in Singapore

Hodder Children's Books
A division of Hodder Headline Limited
338 Euston Road, London NW1 3BH

Contents

Teeth

Teeth! What would we do without them?
People, animals, reptiles and many fish need teeth to cut up and chew food before swallowing it.

A lion has big strong teeth.

A walrus has pointed teeth called tusks.

Snakes have sharp teeth called fangs.

Baby teeth

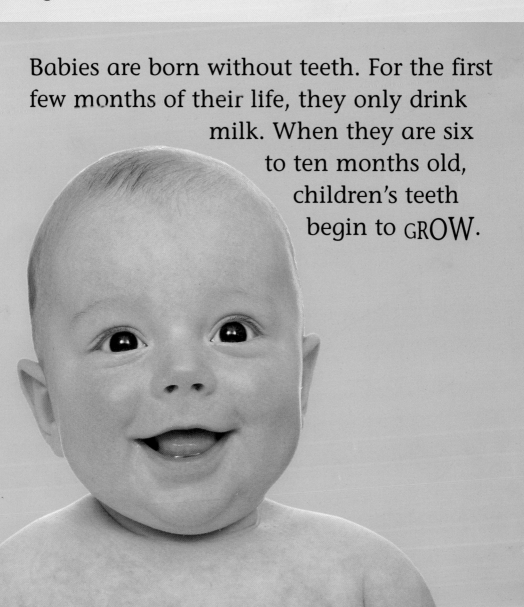

Babies are born without teeth. For the first few months of their life, they only drink milk. When they are six to ten months old, children's teeth begin to GROW.

By the time they
are three years
old, children
have 20 teeth.
They are called
'baby' or 'milk' teeth.

Babies' front
teeth grow
first.

Permanent teeth

When children are about six years old, their 'baby' teeth start to fall out. Slowly, they are replaced with **bigger** and **stronger** teeth.

Children have gaps in their mouths while their grown-up teeth are growing.

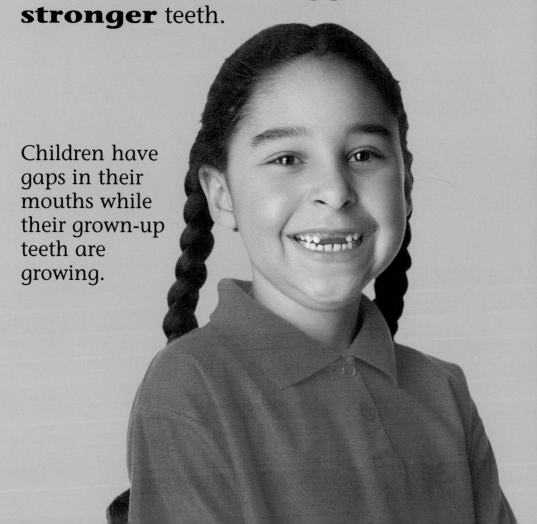

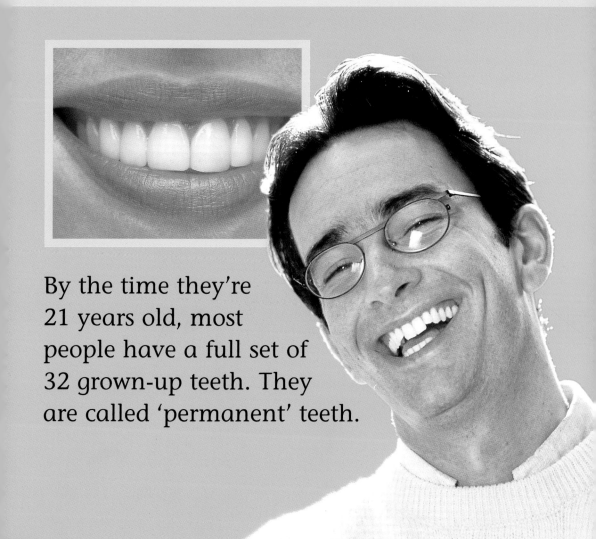

By the time they're 21 years old, most people have a full set of 32 grown-up teeth. They are called 'permanent' teeth.

Meat eaters

Animals which eat only meat have sharp, pointed teeth. Their **strong** front teeth tear and bite at meat. The teeth at the back of their mouths help them to cut through food like a pair of scissors.

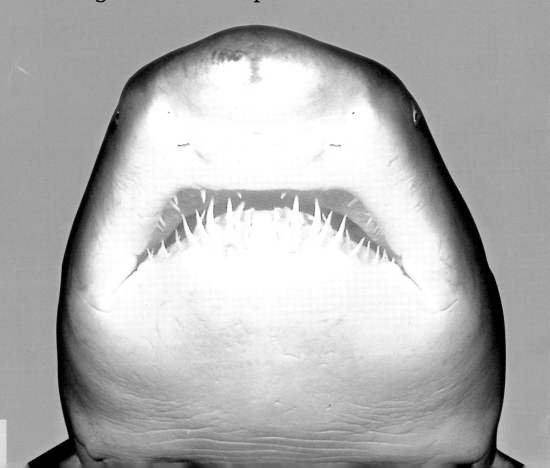

Cats have sharp, long
teeth. They help them
to keep a firm grip
on their food.

Vegetarians

Animals which eat only grass and vegetables have **flat** teeth. Their **strong** front teeth help them to pull up grass and cut through fruit.

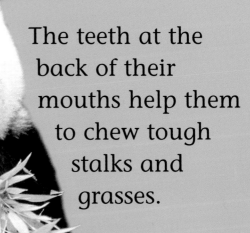

The teeth at the back of their mouths help them to chew tough stalks and grasses.

People can eat both meat and vegetables. So they have both sharp teeth and **flat** teeth.

Squirrels have very strong teeth. They crack nuts open with them.

Human teeth

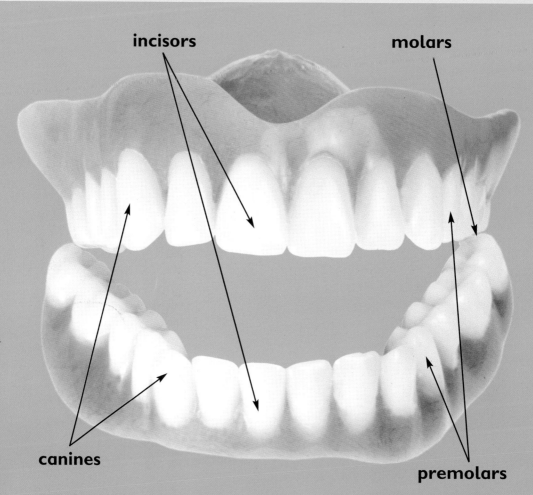

incisors

molars

canines

premolars

Incisors
The eight teeth at the front of people's mouths are called incisors. They help bite and slice through food.

Canines

The four pointed teeth next to the incisors are called canines. They help tear food into smaller bits.

Premolars

The eight teeth next to the canines are called premolars. They help crush and grind food into little bits.

Molars

The eight flat teeth at the back of the mouth are called molars. They chew food into tiny pieces, making it easy to swallow.

Older children often get four more molars in the back of the mouth. These are called 'wisdom teeth'.

Chew on this!

The elephant has the **biggest** teeth in the world – they are called tusks.

Dolphins have more than 200 teeth. They help them to eat lots of fish.

Piranhas are famous for their sharp teeth!

Toothache

Teeth have a white coating called enamel that makes them hard and protects them from getting damaged.

When people eat, SMALL bits of food remain stuck between their teeth. If it is not removed, the teeth get covered in a thin, sticky layer called plaque.

Plaque eats away at the enamel, harming the teeth and causing toothache.

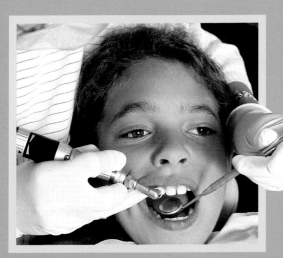

If that happens, people have to go to the dentist, who replaces the damaged enamel with a hard filling.

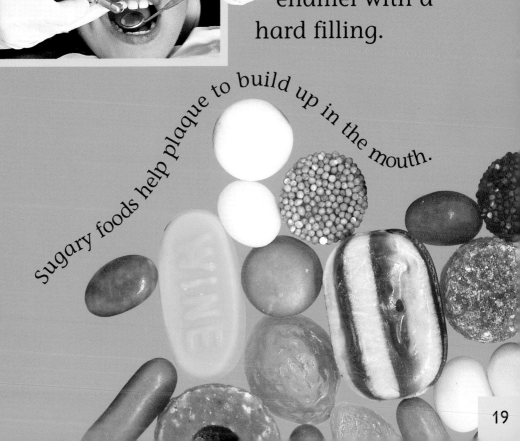

Sugary foods help plaque to build up in the mouth.

Cleaning your teeth with a toothbrush and toothpaste removes plaque. It keeps your teeth nice and shiny too.

Fluoride toothpaste helps to make your teeth stronger.

You should clean your teeth carefully, twice a day. Each tooth must be cleaned in turn, back, front and top.

Don't eat or drink anything except water or milk after you've brushed your teeth at bedtime. And don't have sugary snacks and drinks between meals.

Clean your teeth by moving the brush gently round and round each tooth.

Teeth for life

Your 'permanent' teeth have to last you all your life. That's why you need to look after them.

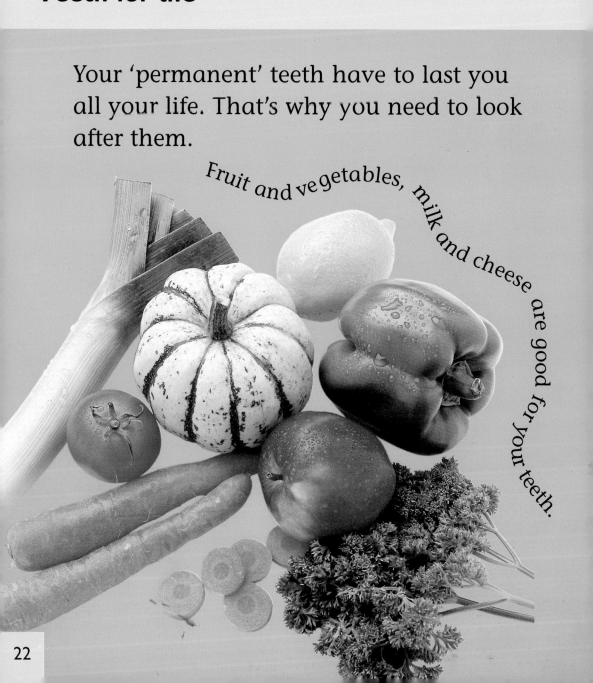

Fruit and vegetables, milk and cheese are good for your teeth.

You should visit the dentist regularly, even if there appears to be nothing wrong with your teeth. You don't want to end up with false teeth!

Now that's food for thought!

Glossary and index

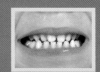

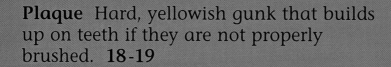